**NATIONAL GEOGRAPHIC**
School Publishing

# Transportation

### Rebecca Sabatani

**PICTURE CREDITS**

Illustrations by Kevin Burgemeestre (4–5, 14–15).

Cover, 1, 9 (above), 11 (left), 12, 13, 16 (above center & below left), Photolibrary.com; 2, 10, 11 (right), 16 (center right), APL/Corbis; 6, 7 (below), 8, 9 (below), 16 (above left, above right, center left & below right), Getty Images; 7 (above), 16 (center), Fotosearch.

Produced through the worldwide resources of the National Geographic Society, John M. Fahey, Jr., President and Chief Executive Officer; Gilbert M. Grosvenor, Chairman of the Board; Nina D. Hoffman, Executive Vice President and President, Books and Education Publishing Group.

**PREPARED BY NATIONAL GEOGRAPHIC SCHOOL PUBLISHING**

Ericka Markman, Senior Vice President and President Children's Books and Education Publishing Group; Steve Mico, Senior Vice President and Publisher; Marianne Hiland, Editorial Director; Lynnette Brent, Executive Editor; Michael Murphy and Barbara Wood, Senior Editors; Bea Jackson, Design Director; David Dumo, Art Director; Margaret Sidlowsky, Illustrations Director; Matt Wascavage, Manager of Publishing Services; Sean Philpotts, Production Manager.

**MANUFACTURING AND QUALITY MANAGEMENT**

Christopher A. Liedel, Chief Financial Officer; Phillip L. Schlosser, Director; Clifton M. Brown III, Manager.

**BOOK DEVELOPMENT**

Ibis for Kids Australia Pty Limited.

Published by the National Geographic Society
1145 17th Street, N.W.
Washington, D.C. 20036-4688

ISBN 0-7922-6049-X

Third Printing 2008
Printed in China

# Contents

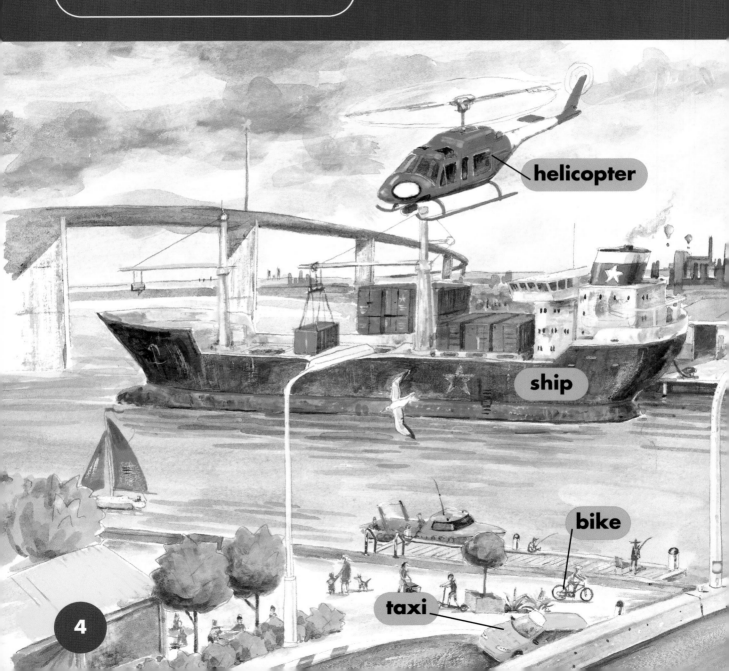

helicopter

ship

bike

taxi

# People go places.
# What kinds of transportation do they use?

plane

train

bus

truck

boat

car

motorcycle

# On Land

People use transportation on land.

People use **bicycles** to go places.

People use **motorcycles** to go places.

People use **cars** to go places.

People use **buses** to go places.

People use **trains** to go places.

People use **trucks** to go places.

9

# In the Air

People use transportation in the air.

People use **planes** to go places.

People use **helicopters** to go places.

People use hot-air **balloons** to go places.

11

# On the Water

People use transportation on water.

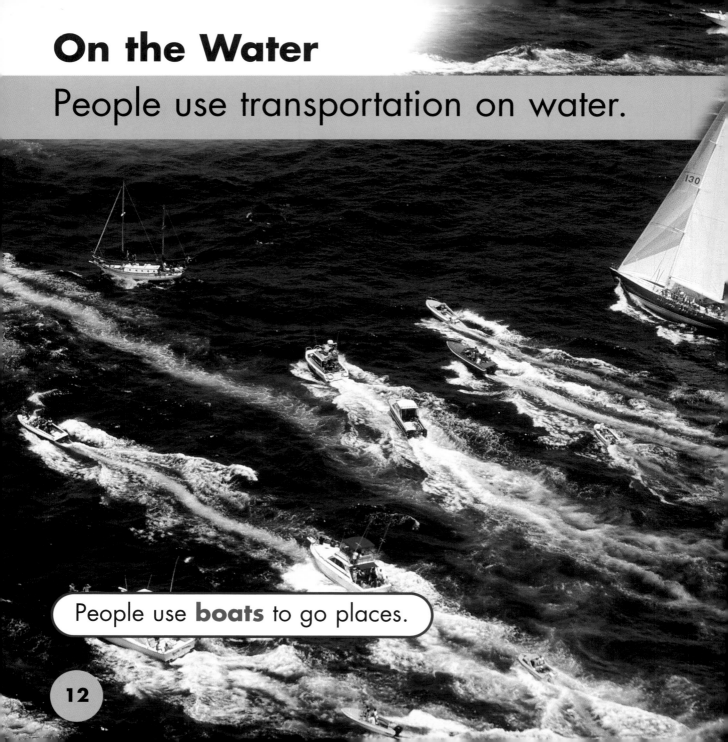

People use **boats** to go places.

People use **ships** to go places.

BIG STUFF

SPORT

sidewalk

river

path

14

# People use transportation.
# What kinds of transportation do you use?

bicycle

boat

bus

car

motorcycle

plane

train

truck

road

bridge

dock

# Picture Glossary

bicycle

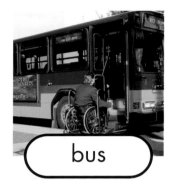
boat

bus

car

motorcycle

plane

train

truck

16